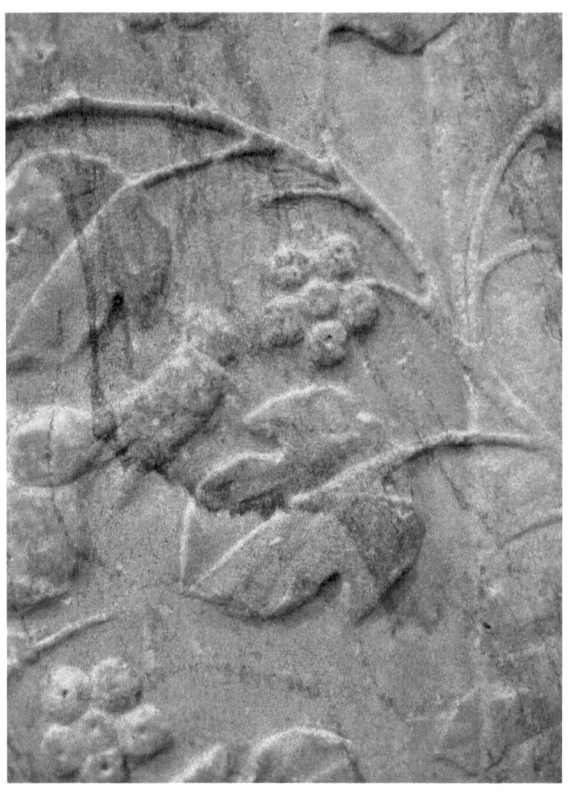

Photos of artworks: D. James Dee
Cover and frontispiece: details of Roman sarcophagii,, photos: Marilyn Henrion

MARILYN HENRION

Reverberations: Keeping Time

"They say that every sound ever made is still reverberating through the universe, however quietly and however distant."

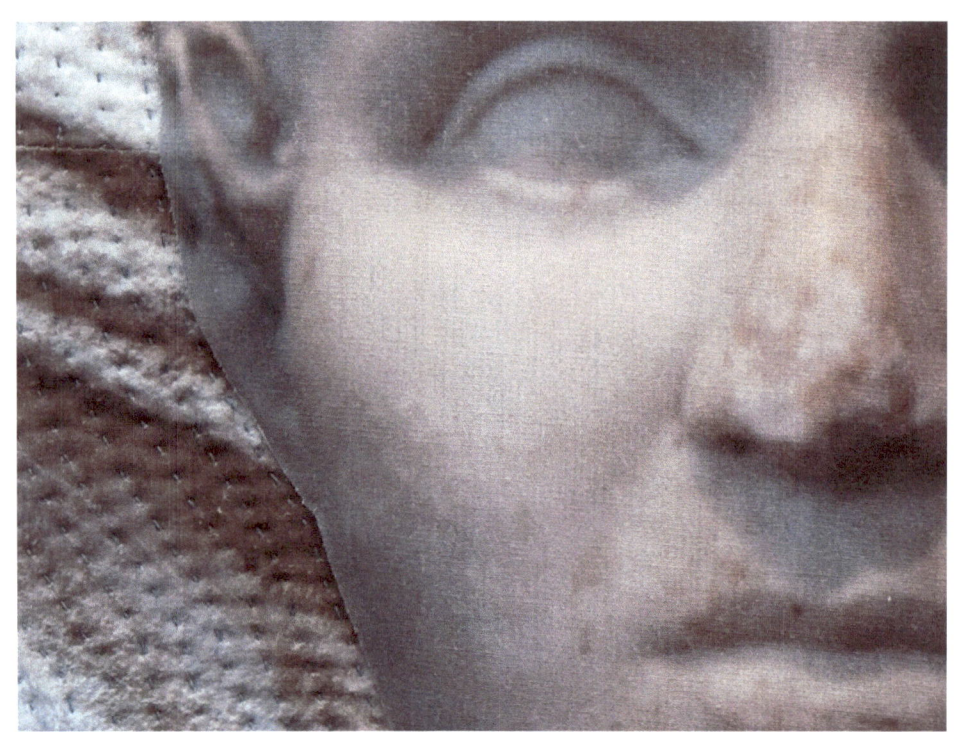

Reverberations: Keeping Time

"They say that every sound ever made is still reverberating through the universe, however quietly and however distant."*

The striving for immortality has been present in civilizations throughout the ages, from cave dwellers to the present. In this quest we have often turned to art to preserve something of ourselves and our values when we are no longer here to speak.

This series of mixed media textile works pays homage to these attempts by focusing on the haunting faces of marble portrait sculptures from ancient Rome at New York's Metropolitan Museum of Art. Marilyn Henrion extracts images from photographs she has taken of these works and prints them onto cloth. Combining these with details from Roman sarcophagi and statues from the same period, she creates textile collages, animating the surfaces with trapunto relief and hand quilting. The presence of Henrion's hand stitching adds yet another layer to the quest for transcendence embedded in the construction of these contemporary works. While the use of representational imagery is a departure from the artist's previously abstract works, the employment of metaphorical reference remains a constant.

* Simon Armitage, "Modeling the Universe: Poetry, Science, and The art of Metaphor"

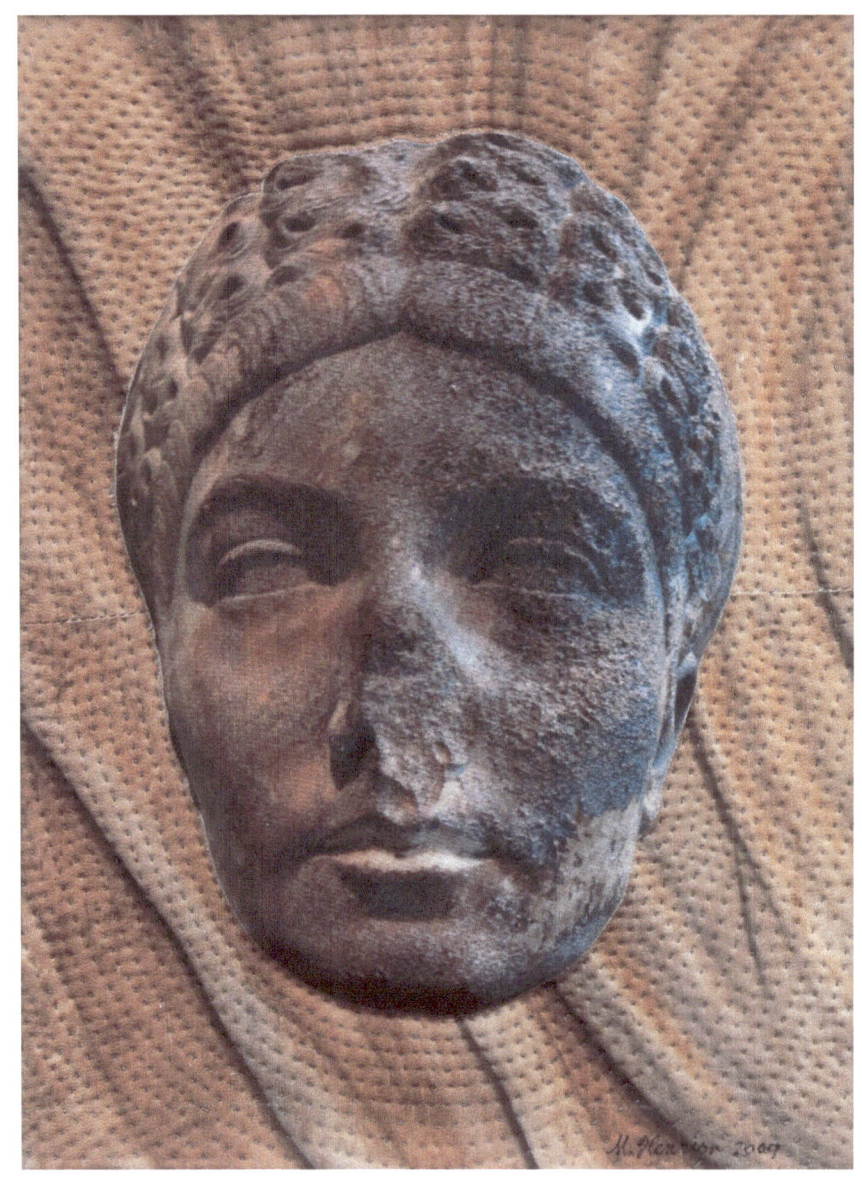

Matidia

12"x9"   digital photography, inkjet printing on cotton, fusing, trapunto, hand quilting

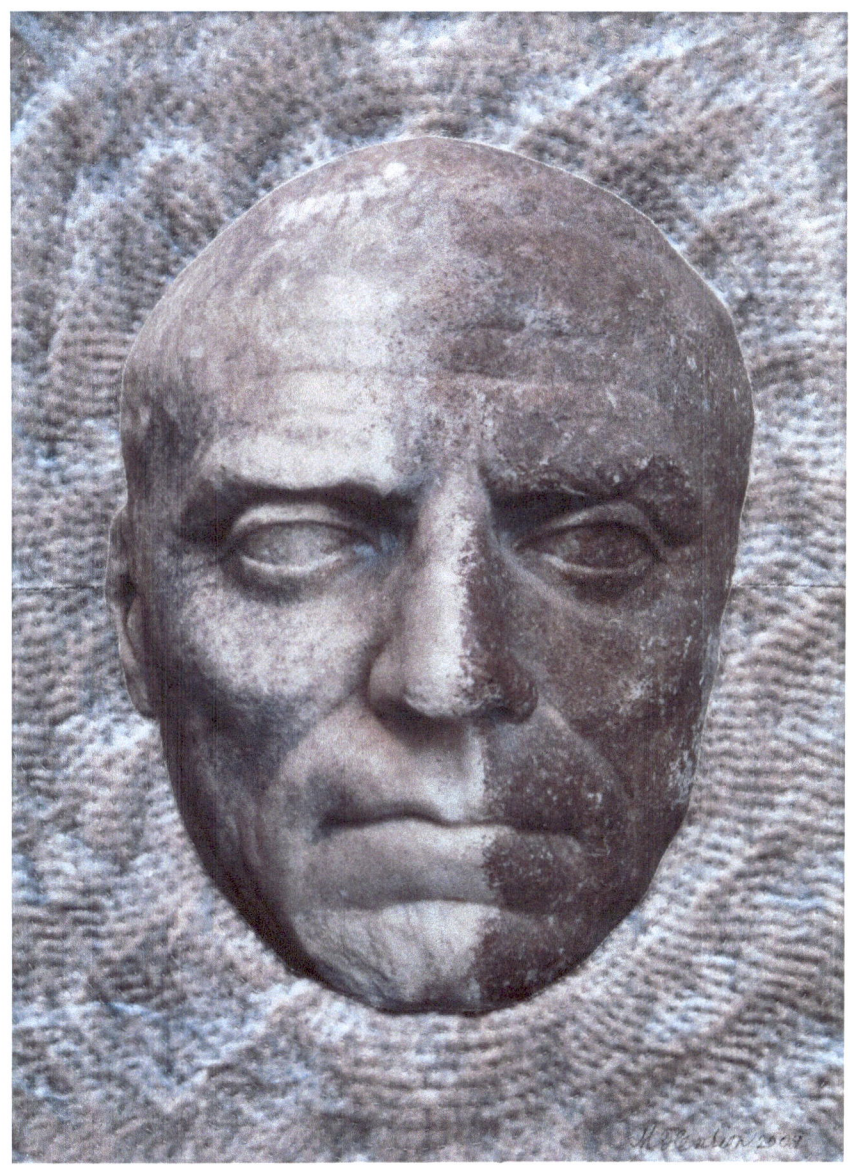

Amandus

12"x9"   digital photography, inkjet printing on cotton, fusing, trapunto, hand quilting

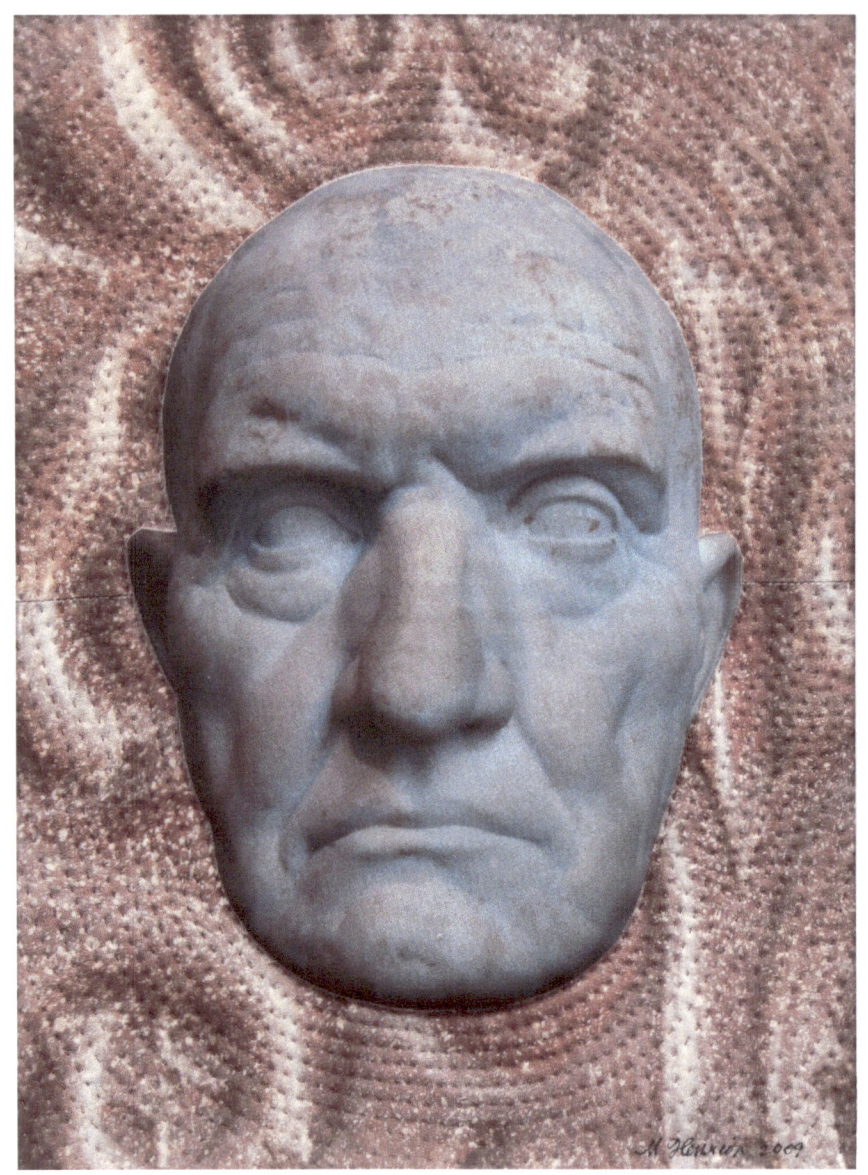

Marius

12"x9" digital photography, inkjet printing on cotton, fusing, trapunto, hand quilting

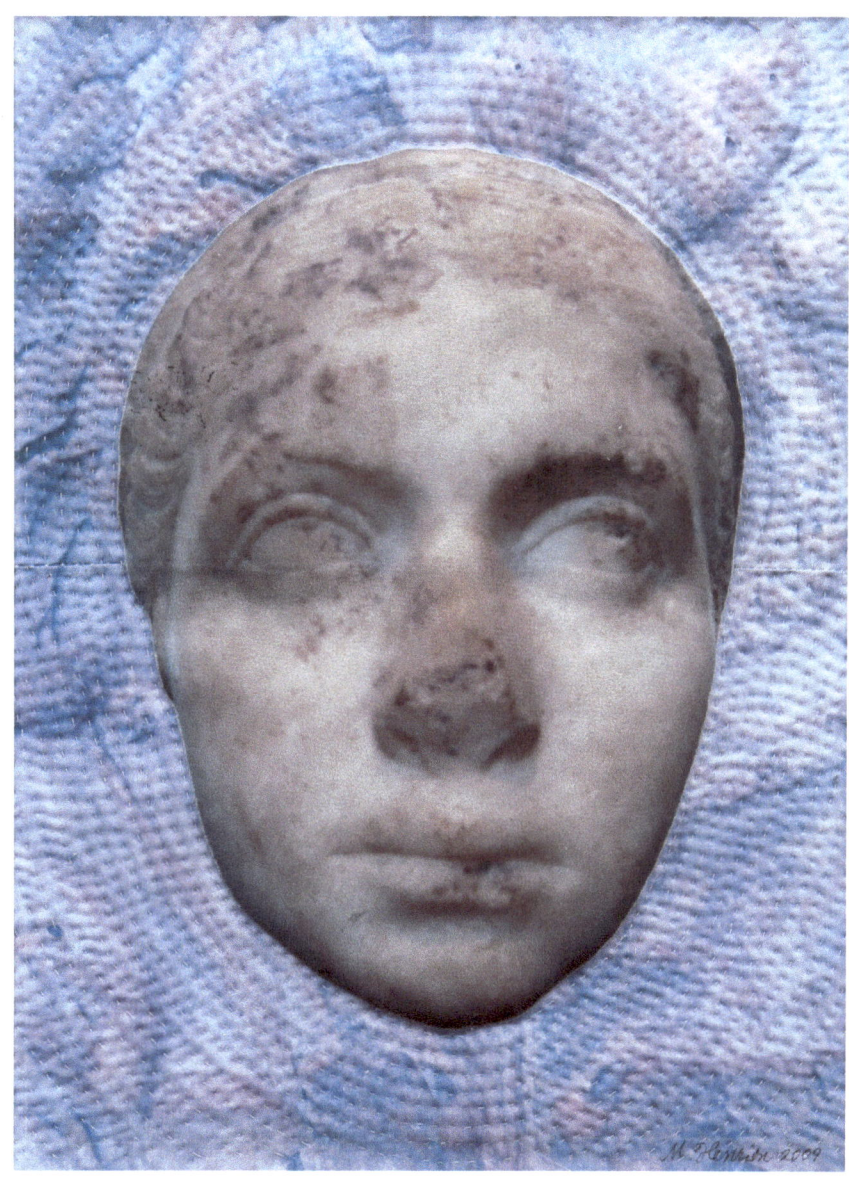

Lucia

12"x9"   digital photography, inkjet printing on cotton, fusing, trapunto, hand quilting

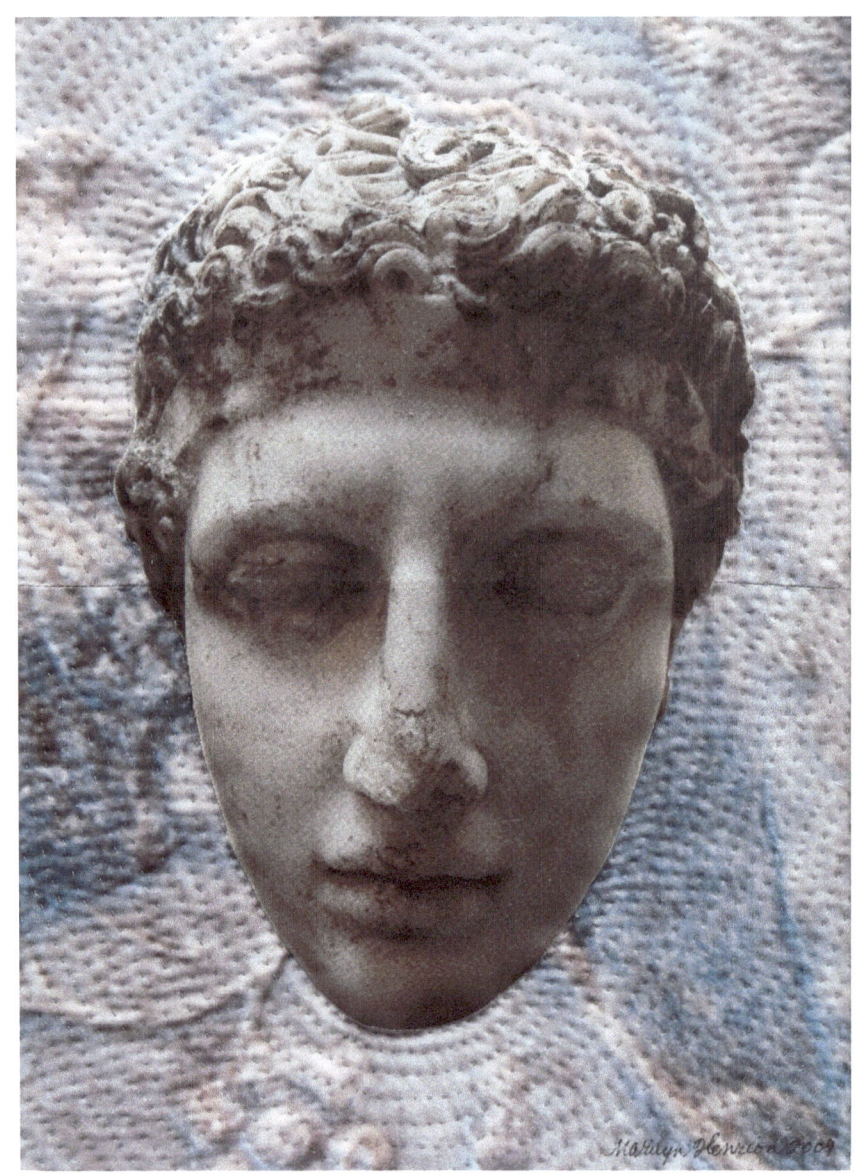

Felicia

12"x9"   digital photography, inkjet printing on cotton, fusing, trapunto, hand quilting

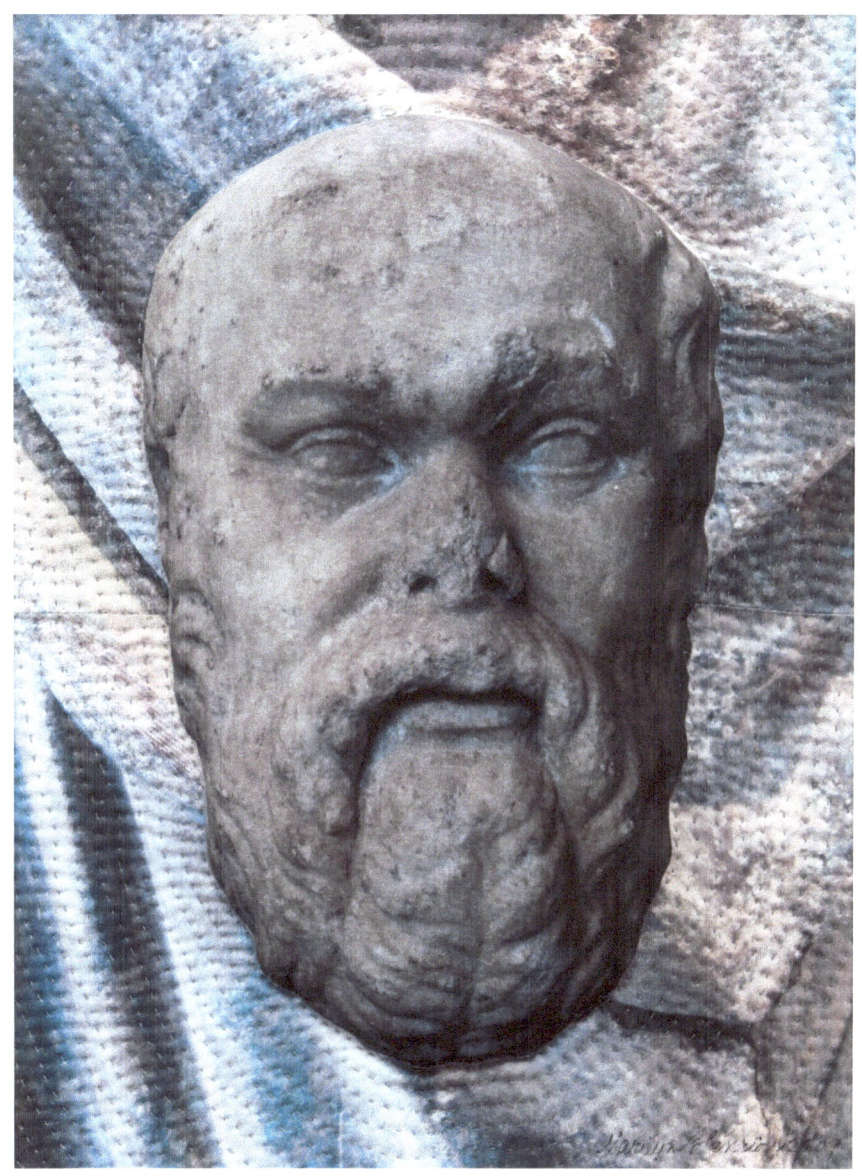

Socrates

12"x9"   digital photography, inkjet printing on cotton, fusing, trapunto, hand quilting

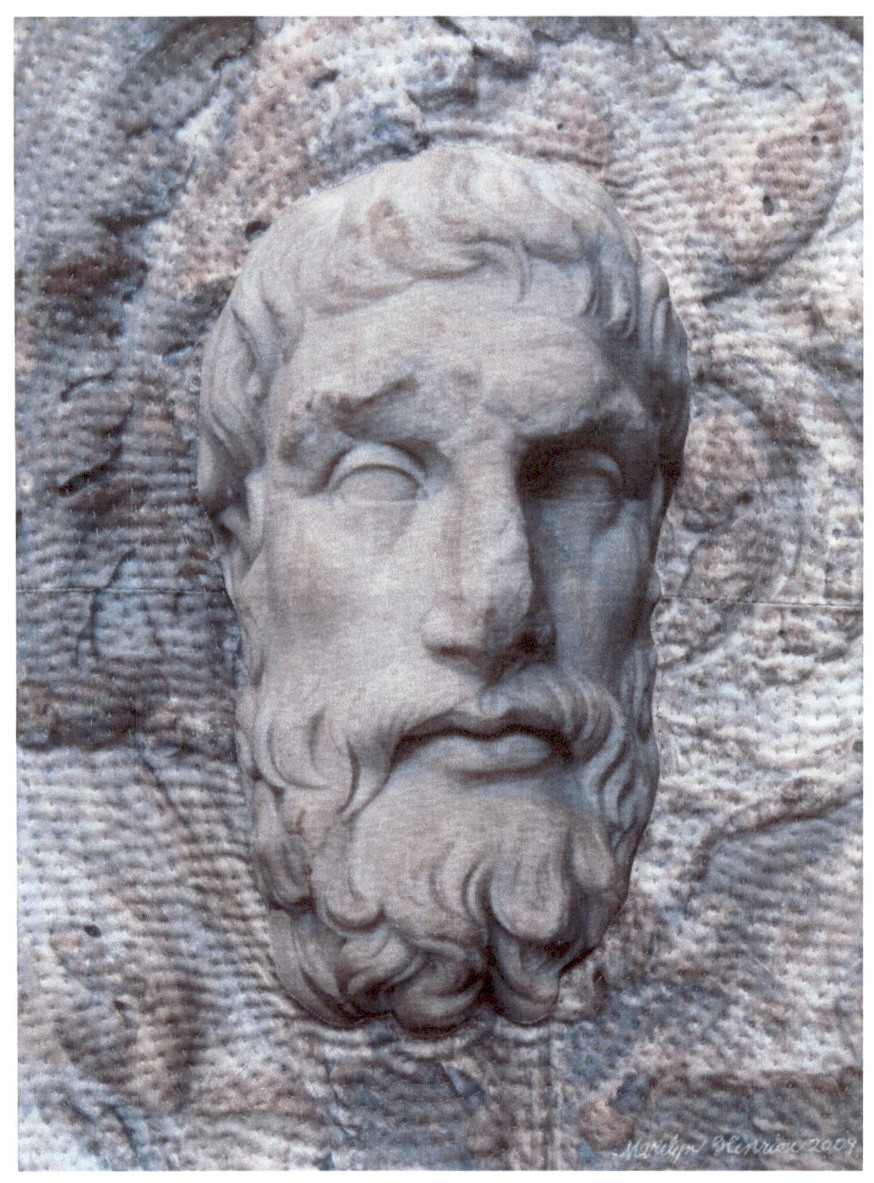

Epikouros

12"x9"   digital photography, inkjet printing on cotton, fusing, trapunto, hand quilting

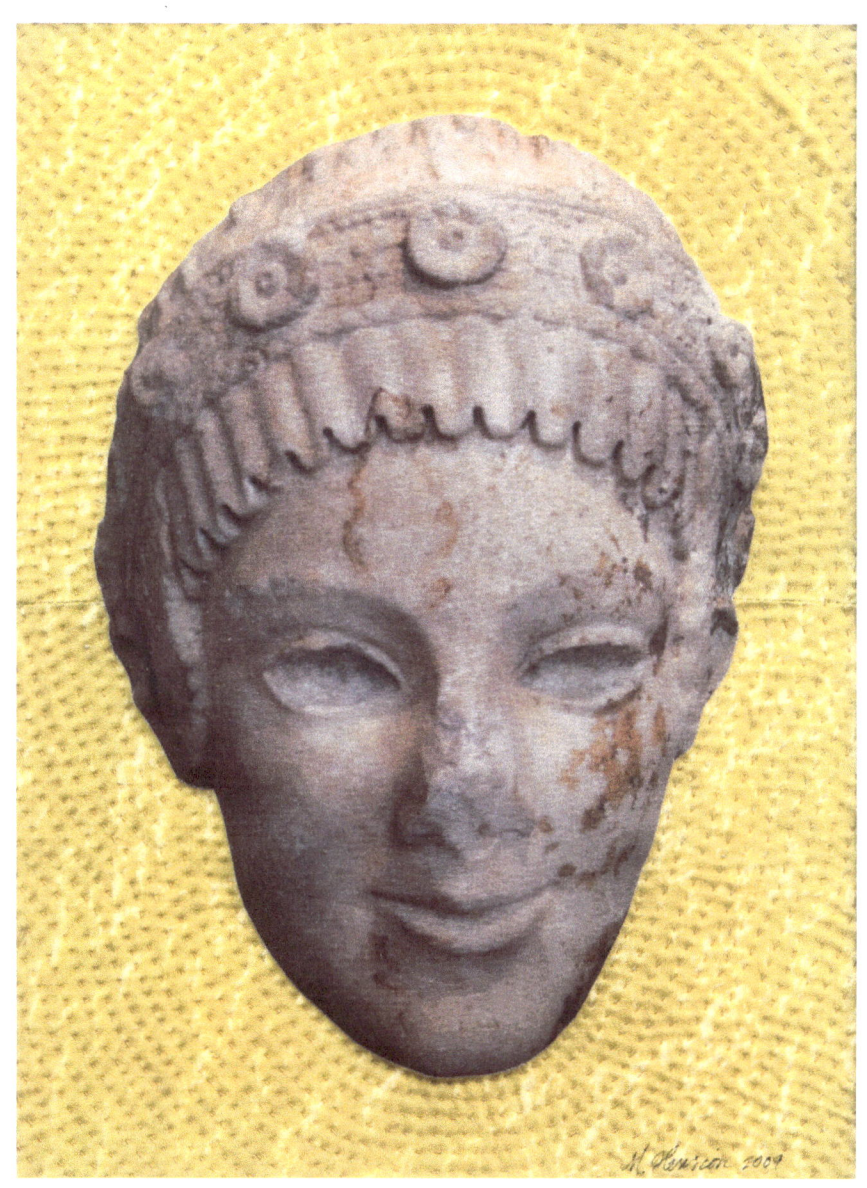

Athena

12"x9"   digital photography, inkjet printing on cotton, fusing, trapunto, hand quilting

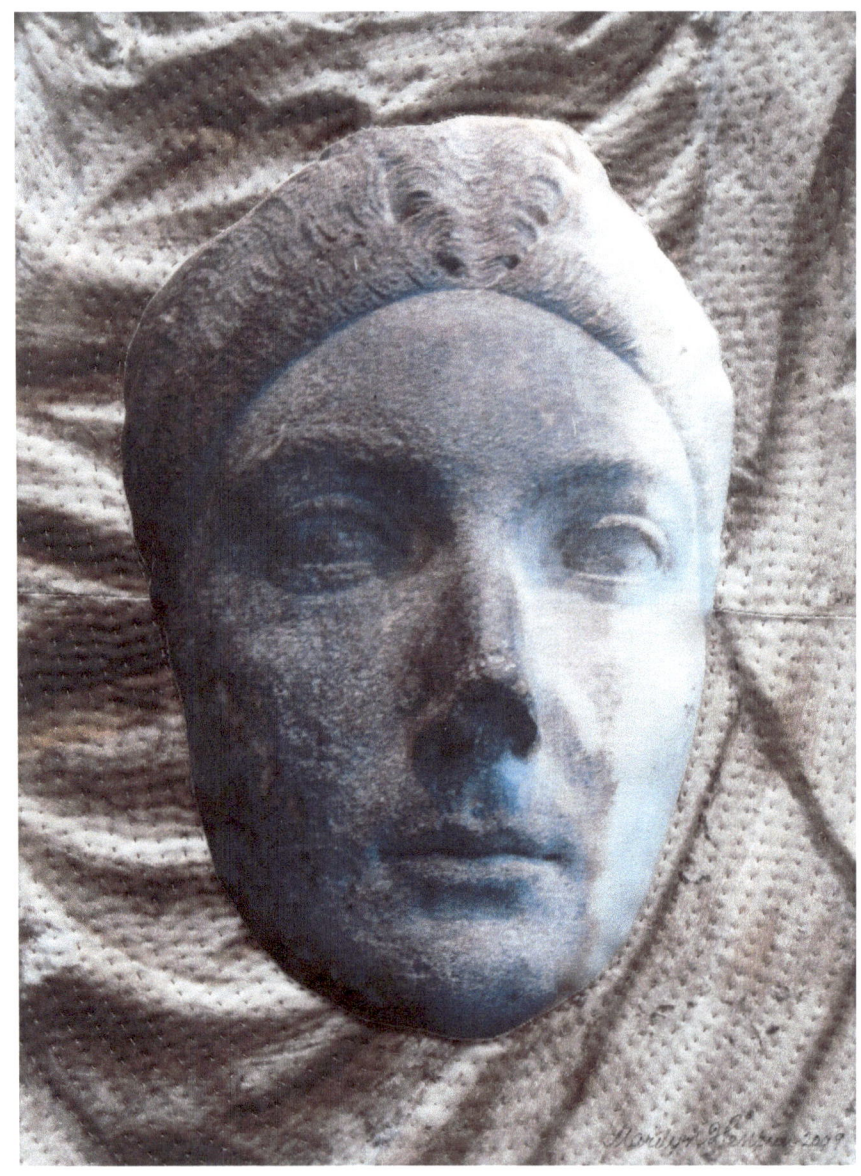

Sabrina

12"x9"   digital photography, inkjet printing on cotton, fusing, trapunto, hand quilting

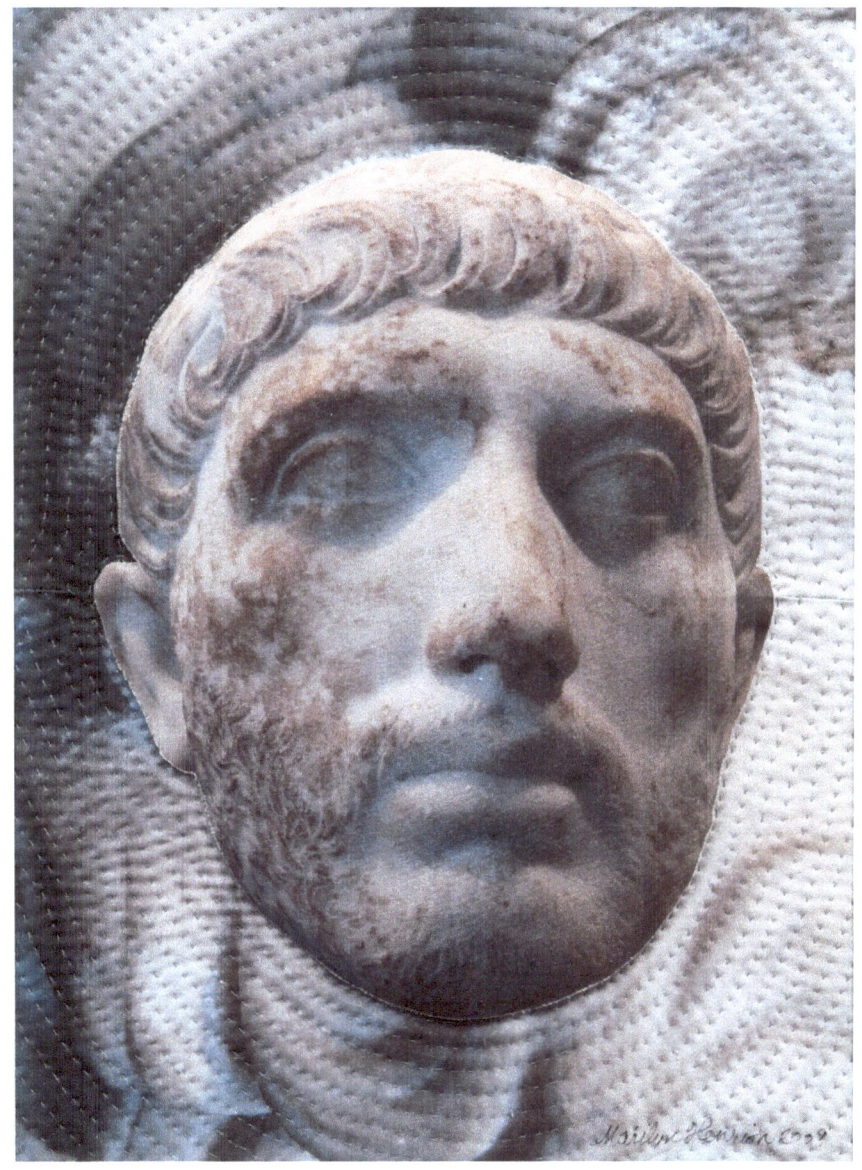

Cassius

12"x9"   digital photography, inkjet printing on cotton, fusing, trapunto, hand quilting

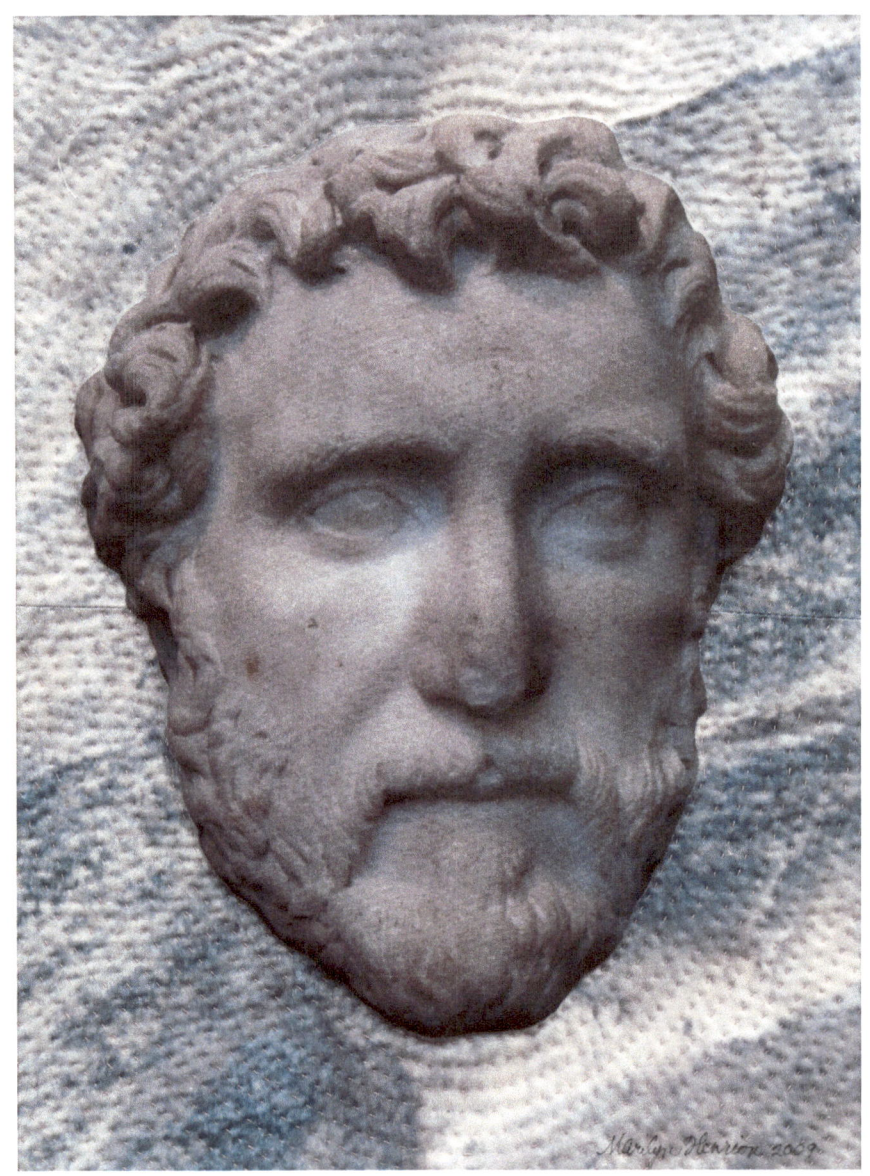

Marcus Aurelius

12"x9"   digital photography, inkjet printing on cotton, fusing, trapunto, hand quilting

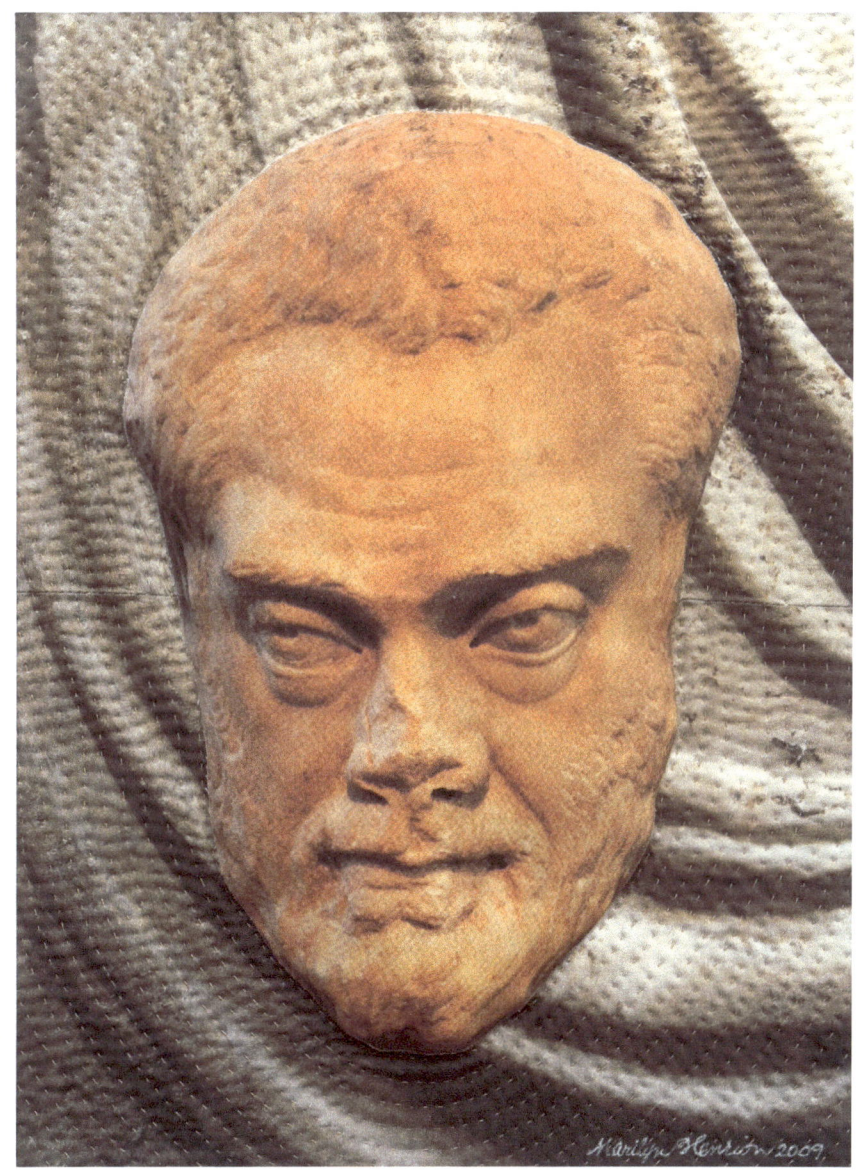

Cato

12"x9"   digital photography, inkjet printing on cotton, fusing, trapunto, hand quilting

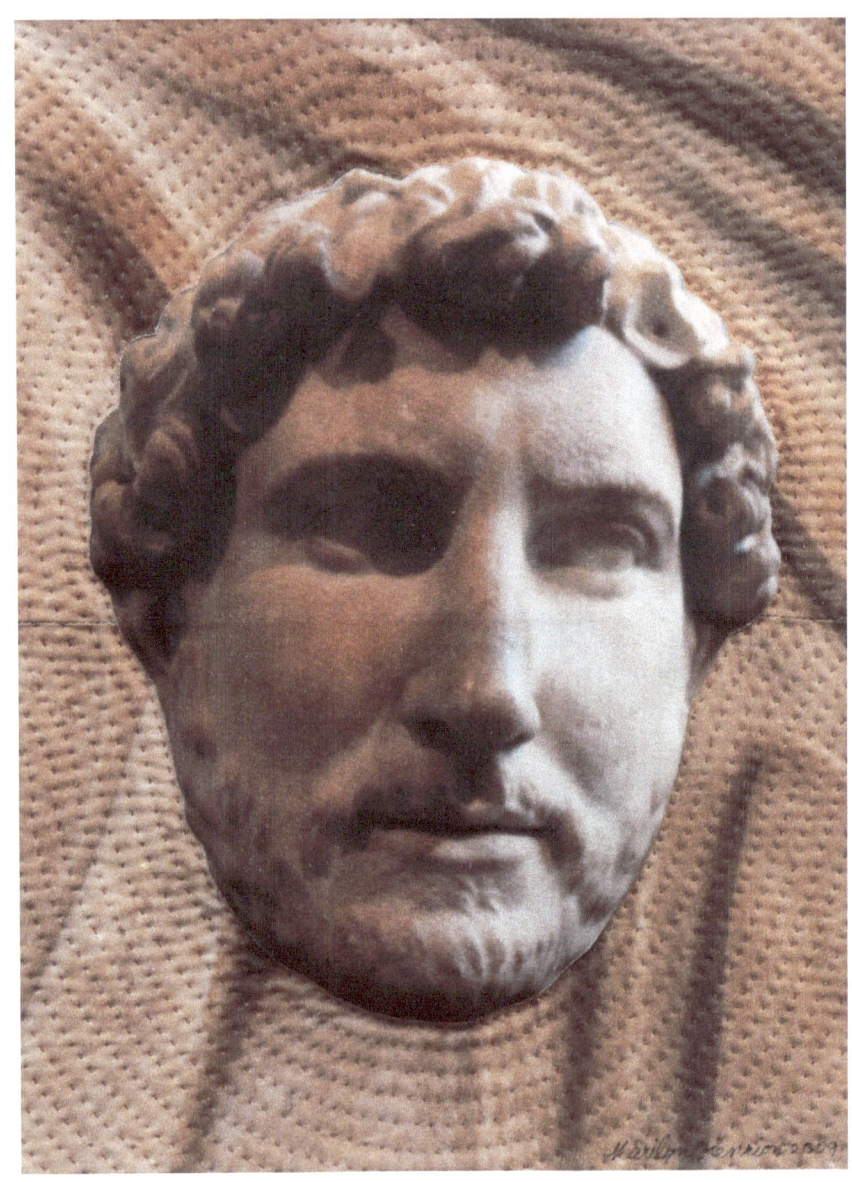

Cornelius

12"x9"   digital photography, inkjet printing on cotton, fusing, trapunto, hand quilting

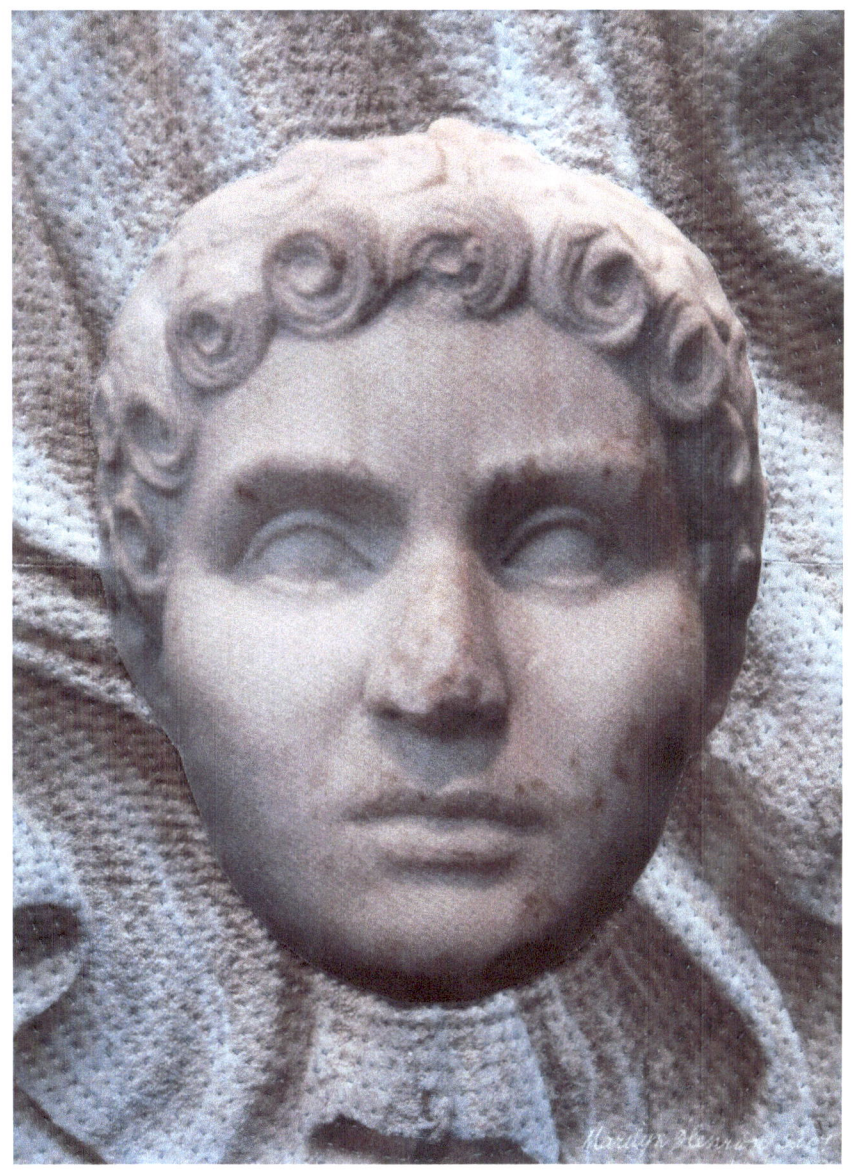

Youth

12"x9" digital photography, inkjet printing on cotton, fusing, trapunto, hand quilting

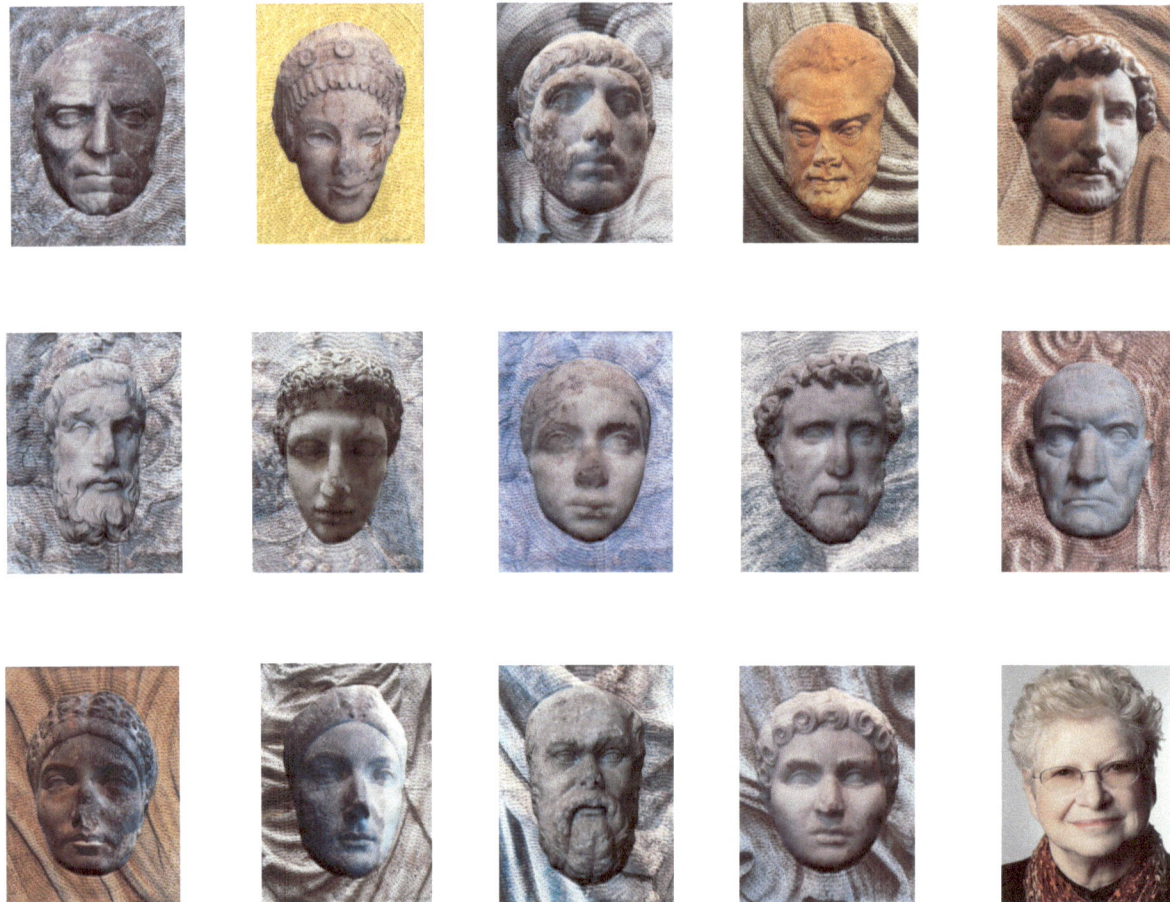

About the Artist

Marilyn Henrion is a graduate of Cooper Union and a life-long New Yorker. her works have been recognized and exhibited internationally. They are included in museum, corporate, and private collections worldwide, including the Museum of Arts & Design in New York, the U.S. Embassy in Pnom Penh, Cambodia, Lucent Technologies, Avaya Corporation, Kaiser Permanente, Carnegie Abbey Country Club, Dana farmer Cancer Institute, SAS Institute, and many more. Among her awards were a New York Foundation for the Arts Fellowship and a grant from the Artslink Foundation for helping to foster excellence in the arts between the U.S. and Russia. Henrion's papers are in the collection of the Smithsonian Institution's Archives of American Art in Washington DC. A complete CD is available on her website, www.marilynhenrion.com.

Acknowledgement

The artist gratefully acknowledges the Metropolitan Museum of Art for providing a never-ending source of enrichment and inspiration to those who enter its doors.